The Economy: Will it be the Market or _____?

Volume Two

By Bill Henderson

The Economy:

Will it be the Market or _____?

Author: Bill Henderson

Publisher:

ICOM Multimedia

ISBN:

978-0-9851022-3-4

Dedicated to the brilliant and classy
Debbie

Special thanks to Phil Yoder for his
creativity and patience

Contents

Foreword

Like most Americans, these are times when you worry about the future. Some of the worries are related to the future of the economy. Since 2008 the economy has not prospered. Economic policies have not reversed the negative economic conditions.

Not many positive situations have been a feature of the Obama administration's economic policies.

So with conditions as they are, the pattern of policies of this administration is important.

In the remaining days of this administration, what economic conditions might be expected to get better or worse?

In the bigger picture is it unlikely that the free enterprise, capitalistic system can be revitalized by more intervention in economic decision making by the government.

Is it likely that modifications to the market system will surface or the market system will be replaced by alternatives such as central government economic planning?

If you do not want change -- that means more of the past Obama policies – or no respite from the decline in the role of markets or even other, more extreme changes.

On the other hand, some few authorities predict a needed strengthening of the market system.

But other prognosticators assume that a larger more complete role of the federal government will be necessary.

A Look Ahead

What is included in this small book is an upgrade of knowledge about the background and the effectiveness of policies based on the market in addition to a review and evaluation of the economic management in the form of central government planning.

Political Roles and Style

It seems that everyone knows that the Obama Care health care insurance program, in written form, is about 2500 to 2700 pages long. That sized document requires a lengthy reading to find out what the policy prescribes.

If you would check with your friends to see if any one of them had ever read some or parts or the entire document, you would probably hear them say that they have not even seen the document – other than a still life photo on the evening news.

It must have taken a lot of people in and out of government a great deal of time and effort to compose and or write such a large piece of legislation. One US Congress person has said that Congress needs to enact the program to '…see what is in it…'.

The program has received a lot of publicity since the Democratic Party controlled Legislature in Washington DC passed the Bill. There have been lots of troubles getting the program off the ground.

No one has really said how long the drafting of the program was in the "works" to become legislation and the law. It is just assumed that whoever was doing the writing - that the Obama administration had employed professional help – probably from Ivy League institutions.

Or maybe it was put together by people who had worked on the 'Hillary Care' program of several years ago. Cynics have said that there was no body in the Legislative services of the Congress smart enough to do the job.

What has become the health care program has encountered several types of issues that have slowed or stymied the program's access to the people.

Who seems to want such a complex and expensive program?

The inexorable drive to the left is an expected move by socialists' ideologues like Obama whose long term drive is the transformation of the economy.

The cynics have said the program takes the form of more and more government control.

It can be argued that the program was never expected to "work."

But it was a step in a long and clever strategy to get rid of the private insurance industry and move to the "single payer" structure, that is having only the government providing any insurance options available to the public.

What a crazy idea - that the complex program was designed to fail.

Why? What sense does that make?

It makes a lot of sense if you are to assume that the intention was to end competitive capitalism and/or *end the private sector control of the economics processes.*

The Obama administration is hell bent on having more and more control provided by the central government.

It is axiomatic that Obama wants to continue to restructure the US economy.

He is a leftist who is predictable and a stereotypical Socialist in terms of his economic model of the economy.

In economic literature there is ample historical information of the preferred structure of a socialist economic system.

One salient feature of those economies is economic mandates and laws from the center of political power to mandate economic allocation and structural decisions.

Obama, as a devotee leftist, typically espouses ideas as concepts about the need to develop a means to transform the US economy into a typically centralized type with direction and control from the elitist groups in Washington regimes. *This will 'move the economy' along a direct series of mechanisms which eliminate the formerly established competitive, capitalistic market system.*

It is a given, that options and opportunities are created by the current ruling political party (regimes of the Democrat Party, controlled Congress,) with leverage provided by media.

The media will continue to be the source of public support for Obama, with installed and implemented media designed for ill-informed voters and journalists.

The move toward central control of the economy might not seem to be very dramatic. The controlled economies will have the precedent character of what might be a form or type of centralized control. But the exact form, of course, is now unknown.

It may be somewhat helpful to have a look at types of centralization and economic planning elsewhere and in the past.

Expected Economic Impacts

Like most Americans, these are times when you *should* worry about the future.

One reason is that Obama has indicated that he would use executive orders and his pen to get what he wanted - from a Congress which he viewed as unproductive.

The great bill-stopping machinery in the Congress over the past several years was the work of Harry Reid. Reid may be gone in the near future. The Republicans never figured out a socio-political approach that prevented them from being labeled as impotent. Check the numbers.

Some would argue that the Obama administration national politics verifies that he does not plan to withdraw from maintaining an active role with no withering after 2016.

After Obama

So how will future adjustments and future influences work out?

Even if Obama no longer has actual nominal legislative power, his influence through the pre-election period and beyond will be a dominant factor.

The assumption is that Obama's mandated changes in the health care may simply affirm that he would like to stay on as President for another year to make sure that Obama Care would be continued via Obama leadership.

But when he would opt to leave - a suitable successor is mandated.

To secure an extension, the person selected would be relied upon to support Obama's legacy in the Presidency.

It is likely that there will be more and more comments about the Clintons. Their role is suspect - too pragmatic - too egocentric - too old - different political & personal ambitions – to be considered for very long.

Obama's wife – Michelle - is a logical choice.

But think of the days ahead of the election with a Michelle O. candidacy.

The country may be faced with another Obama law change - even more heavy handed than the Obamacare mandate changes in 2013 and 2014.

Future Change

To "fix" or make operational the Obama Health Care structure and administration is that one goal of the administration is to dissolve the private insurance sector - to be replaced by the government single player devices.

There has been little evaluation of what the demise of the rational private insurance companies will mean to the general economy.

Insurance policies have been made financially secured by the insurance companies.

In order to meet the actuarial requirements - a traditional means of saving for many – for many US families.

Insurance policies have been a useful and important option for hedging future family and personal financial risks.

As to economic impact - there is not now any similar type of risk reduction option for the future without the insurance option now existing.

With the availability of liquidity in the hands of the insurance commonly available for the traditional role of insurance company functions, what voids are created?

The personal savings in the purchase of insurance policies constitutes a flow of liquidity to insurance companies to be managed and invested.

The flow of funds sent to insurance companies, in turn, is put into money market as a type of investment.

With elimination of the private sector value and the single payer/mandates, the insurance companies may also opt to buy government debt as an investment into the system as business or personal financial flows.

It all depends on the media and what it tries to convey to the ignorant and ill-informed about a justification for the extension of the Obama legacy.

No hope from the media in slowing down the pell-mell rush to push the country further to the left.

It is not clear what steps could be taken by whom to prevent or invalidate such a move. No one seemed to know what to do about the arbitrary date changes that made in the mandates in 2013 and 2014.

Heavy duty future worries are thus related to the future. The Administration needs to be able to shut off more revelations about behavioral activities.

Some of that information may be additions to the Administration's more interference with the individual freedom that most Americans favor and treasure.

Of course the socio-political scenario created by the Administration will follow the same genre of Obamacare.

That included fabrication of the program, outright lying by the Democratic Party spokespeople and creating a veil of ignorance which prevented people from finding out what was in the legislation.

Time on His Hands

Some few people would respond to all of these future changes by saying "Look at the calendar." The year of the next election is too close for Obama to be able to implement his leftist thrust.

Not many positive situations have been features of the Administrations' polices that Obama has used for economic problem solving. Or there may be efforts where economic planning by the central government in the next years is exactly what is needed to change the economy.

But what would be advanced politically to make economic conditions to get better or worse.

In the larger picture, is it likely that the free enterprise, capitalistic system can be revitalized?

Or is it more likely that modifications to the market system will erode and be replaced by alternatives such as central government economic planning?

Planning is the Obama legacy.

Some Review OR Repeats of Good Stuff

Remember this topic as a section in earlier pages?

Well, anyway look at it again. This is important stuff.

So how would you as an author go about presenting the information which is necessary TO PRESENT TO THE UNIFORMED POTENTIAL READER ABOUT CONDITIONS THAT ARE REAL but not perceived as real with the under educated - or in the "analysis" process of well-educated or generally considered "intelligent people?

This is a real issue because people who are uninformed do not read or enquire about the topics which would bring about a 'tick-up' in their learning curve?

Or how is it that a writer might productively reach the informed potential readers that seem able to understand economic processes and design a pattern of substantial information for the nonreader?

Of course this dilemma is amplified at the other end of the spectrum by facing the issue of how to defuse misconceptions and interpretations, and analysis of public policies, when the political views distort views in terms of solutions-oriented policies - or which are designed to exacerbate the economic issues rather than foster improvements in the economy?

This group of quasi-informed readers cannot or do not know how to trace the impacts and dimensions of policy implementations.

And this group relies on sources of evaluation which are politically and ideologically biased and lack understanding of the counter intuitive impacts of economic policy on the roles played by consumers and investors in a market economy.

But do not get the idea that the ignorance quotient is the characteristic of low income, poorly educated groups or in higher income well educated groups.

The ignorance issues are vested in all socially structured peoples in the economy and concentrated on by the media, news reporters, and the majority members of the U.S. Congress.

One current down side economic policy issue in the Western World is the lack of understanding of the economy.

Another issue is the focus on personal hedonism rather than the common good.

Another issue is the lack of understanding of the absence of humility in the motive and direction for economic well-being.

Another issue is the internalized, material benefits that dominate people in sorrow and people who are designing ineffective and destructive requirements for actions which try to prohibit personal participation in the sorrows.

Freedom of participation in the issues does not require direction from a secular government but requires understanding of the ways by which the impacted are guided to personal actions and behavior which may ease and not amplify the sorrows of the world.

A widespread and high ranking issue in the US is the widespread acceptance of ignorance as the basis for personal acceptance of responsibility for improving the quality of life of the decision makers or players in both the private sector and public sector of economic ideas and assumptions about material well-being of all of the economic players.

But more than that, the economic players do not seem to be mentally equipped to follow consequences of ineffective and counterproductive ill designed centralized concepts and/or ideas which are designed to amplify rather than reduce uncertainty or strengthen the economy.

From a practical effort, there is a common need for common sense and rationality of concepts which applied to economic roles of the private and public sector will bring improved economic wellbeing for every one as "economic players" in the system.

It is an issue that people do not understand economic processes and also that people who are said to understand those economic process are biased, short sighted and generally lack the knowledge or other abilities to trace though the effects of the economic actions that follow from their economic irrationality.

A different type of economic allocation system describes how resources are to be used.

Rather than have market forces determine the distribution, allocation or use of the nation's resources, some bureaucratic agency is in place to design, implement and control the use of resources. *These agencies are/were typically described as "planning" agencies.*

Planning and state owned enterprises occur with or without a democratic political system. State owned resources can be in place without planning.

Planning somehow worked marginally better if there was state ownership of resources.

Democracy and state ownership can take place without a planning mechanism.

There are many different structures for economic organizations.

Durability of State Roles

A contemporary research effort to find examples of central government economic planning will lead to very few countries or cases. .

A survey of planning which is not historically focused in the first decades of the 21st Century produced a few contemporary examples of centrally planned economies. The fall of the Berlin wall and reforms in the USSR in the last decades of the 20th Century brought the demise of the interest and use of central government economic planning to all of the former Russian states.

There was a rush to dump the Soviet influence and control and a rush to "go right" toward a revived capitalism. There were no lengthy debates in any east Europe countries about retaining any vestiges of the old planning controls.

A review pointed out non planning interest in careful creative programs. Issues related to population pressures and the environment and other issues whether the particular features of the proposals are workable, or can be implemented or have a basis in reality of possible outcomes consistent with needs as benefits to the general public benefactors.

Concerns with Economic Planning

If you did a survey of people asking, "what about China and Russia?" What about planning in those left regimes today?

In the case of China, the various Party politics play a huge role in rationalizing the pressures for economic controls, economic progress and rapid economic growth. Legislation and rules based of solutions to the economic issues dominate rather than the historical ideological anachronism of the former Mau regimes. There is continued interest in mechanisms or devices that meet government needs to preserve the devices or foundation which government controls flexible enough to manage a flurry of economic exigencies.

Thus, leftist rationales permit the availability of expanding foreign trade, participation in world financial markets and acceptance of the need for an improving standard of living for the general populace.

For example, foreign companies are allowed but limited to 50% of the business. The issues for which academicians have developed concerns dominate all decision making about economic programs or about moving back or away from government control. Investment controls are a general way to steer or limit. It is a feeling that is important and not cause or effect. To manage accumulation speeds up the process and makes it less important for Obama's unknown plinth of somebody's ideology. The availability of data or application of any program mix feature of a particular program or legislation business expansion. The role of the Party is important in dealing with economic relationships with foreign companies and nations. China is under great crisis. So what does that mean in *terms* of the days ahead and economic planning by the central government regarding rapid growth with limited resources? Urbanization issues including infrastructure and environmental issues dominate economic decisions.

Russia must continue to deal with its internal and national security and use economic designs and ideas to strengthen the long forthcoming conflict over relations with pressure to be interested an in getting a bigger share of benefits from the government as well as the necessity of working or training for increases in output or real income.

And about Russia—the bottom line—is vigorous pragmatism guiding domestic and international; strategies to strengthen largess for the movers and shakers of the economy are Russia's effectiveness as a world power. That focus means an interest in economic policies, controlled by the majority parties in making Russia a place where ingenuity, creativity, clever management and financial strategies foster rapid development. Increasing political pressures in assuring safe Asian borders will dominate Russian interest for many years in the future.

Some Country Case Examples

Policy issues were related to shifting power in the Party rather than in worker interest or problems with difficulties with the regimes' practical impact on the economy. And to find policies which may cause some economic improvements. So how bad do things need to get of be and what possibilities of policy are open short of central economic planning?

Or what level of frustration impacts the regime to move to more heavy-handed action?

--Whether or not planning is simply an ideologue symbol may bring economic was concerned that the party apparatus would lead to insight into whether or central planning may in fact bring the results desired in the way of economic change or provide only a superficial ideological plinth of leftist ideas—but which have little or no clarification of basic principles useful in directing an economy.

The use of economic planning gets written into economic history primarily because of the need for some type of economic organization in economies which impact the enduring economic crisis.

For practical purposes that determines the power of political parties or political ideology. Does planning do what it was expected to do by the advisors and designers of the format? Not necessarily so - but rather to the impact on the political parties or regimes which favored the establishment of the planning system. Planning was a means to strengthen or achieve national security. The types of planning were many and diverse. The differences reflected the institutional and political structure the political machinations and status that illustrated the socio-economic - political heritage of the different nations.

Planning initiatives took place in democracies and parliament and oligarchy systems. Some planning was indicative-that is implied, sent to the governing parties by the heads of State.

The success of planning was and is a function of highly centralized or de-centralized power structures and with strong and less strong penalties for failure to comply with mandates and regulations by the state or planning bureaucracy.

The durability of planning models and structures was and continues to be tied not to the idea of planning or the form of planning or most important - not to the success of planning in ameliorating the economic crisis.

State planning was in use in Russia from the WWI through the next several decades. Russian planning interest as a durable issue involved many serious challenges to the interpretations of Lenin by Russian functionaries.

So starting after World War one, the Marxist ideologies were set up as a diversified area - with resources and a talented labor supply kind of ideological cloud hanging over an economy which was agricultural when there was need for increases in food and fiber and manufactured goods. There was period of ideological debates in the 1920-21 period in Russia. Names associated with ideas in the period were Bukharin and Stalin.

Issues like the workers control of industry, the use of industrial trusts, questions of when should the state wither away, were all raised. That was period which became known as "the end of utopianism." Bukharin was able put together something called "new economic policy" which alluded to Lenin's last ideas in the thirties which was a dominant economic issue for the USSR. Still in the category of an underdeveloped economy, the challenges of Debates continued for a period about issues raised by Stalin and Trotsky. Bukharin was a non-functionary. Incidentally, Trotsky escaped to Mexico and was concerned with the direction of the Party and politicians and feared that there would be a shift of power away from farmers and factory workers to Party functionaries.

A period when there was a struggle between the Party Left and Right. The right lost. Bukharin of the right was disposed and Stalin began his careful but slow movement to centralize his power in the party and/or the Left. The NEP lasted through most of 1920s. By 1927 Stalin had strengthen his position. Bukharin was a non-functionary. The trials and stabilization of the Stalin leftist regime occurred. The rise of Nazi aggression of Stalin and Trotsky continued with Trotsky escaping to Mexico. Incidentally he was later murdered by a Stalinist. Bukharin was eventually arrested, put on trial in a famous court fight over ideological - was found guilty and shot.

The debates within the Party continued through the 1930s with various reforms and structural administrative changes. Russia was still basically an undeveloped economy at the outbreak of WWII.

With the aid of the US Lend Lease Program, a skilled and talented labor force and huge agricultural areas for large grain supplies was created. Hungary provided some wartime economic needs were met by Russia.

The end of the war changed, in maximum fashion, the role of Russia European and World politics. The war was carried out at high cost to the Russian. The settlements agreements between Roosevelt, Churchill and Stalin produced a new map of Europe and a sharp increase in the role of Russian economic connections with Europe.

The Russians set up Communist Party control in newly acquired Balkan and Baltic areas.

Russia got partial control - including state ownership, confiscation of property and assets. The regimes undertook a nationalization program with involved public transport, medical services, nationalization of companies and mines. The Communist Parties were under direct control of the Russian politicians. Economic and political decisions although vested in the local parties allowed for no deviation from the Russian edicts.

The war was won at high cost and sacrifice for Russians. Post recovery was aided by the distribution of countries between the West and the East.

Russia acquired the Balkans, and Baltic countries and parts of Germany and control over parts of Austria. These annexed areas started its growing plans in a real sense in Russia after the move of the economy to the Left.

Crisis of the government and the working through of what resources and a talented labor supply was took the form of economic organization compatible with the Marxists/Leninist interpretation.

Post World War Two Impact

The satellite countries were integrated economically into the Soviet planning models. New sources of skilled labor and economic resources were adjuncts to the Russian resources base.

Poland added more seaborne connections with its ports. Poland provided a bureaucratic approach which was a more practical administration. This was followed with variations, after WWII, with the British Labour government and in Russia. Slovakia became a region of heavy industrialization in the NW and SE. There were good agricultural lands in the central part of the country. Local regimes confiscated property and assets were state acquired. The planning system of the indicative type was favored by the Labour Party. There was nationalization of mines, transport, and companies, as the USSR engulfed the satellite countries. A model of prolonged debates was established in eastern Europe.

Of course, the Soviets ran the legal systems and controlled the press. The controlled court system was used to thin out and control any perceived threats to the regime.

During this period, east and south European activity by the Reds were forays into state planning in other parts of Europe. Forms of central planning spread through the economies of several States/s in the post-war two period.

Great Britain, in a post war Recovery effort, moved to the left fostered by the Labour Party. There was a wave of nationalization involving transport, mines, factories and other former private services. The left moves were very controversial. The effects on economic growth and recovery were key in the economy, but were not hidden or bound by the left political ideologies. They were also controversial. Given a period of experience with the larger role of government, Britain moved back to the right under Thatcher.

Sweden turned to increase State controlled narrow short term projects more than in any other cases of Post War II examples. Sweden and Finland increased the government control after the War. It was identified as a "socialist state" with property nationalized and increased leftist institutional changes, as the arguments for moving and economy like the US further to the left and to the adoption of central government. Economic planning points to a couple of interesting local designs of the government roles in their post war recovery. French planning was notably more successful in its use of bright, skilled approach more pragmatic approach and efforts. Germany and Italy were overtly pragmatic in designing economic policies which took maximum advantage of the cooperation with the West.

Another Look at Planning Applications

A short conclusion about other nations' using economic planning. Central government planning is not "the way to go" for most countries in the world. So why should the US - particularly the US and Obama move to an economic control system that in and of itself is not functional as economic policy? The short answer is some version of leftist ideology and its related power to move the country to the left is the rational for Obama interest in central government planning.

The Administration
A Background of Planning Uses

State planning was in use in Russia from the WWI through the next several decades. Russian planning interest as a durable issue involved many serious challenges to the interpretations of Lenin by Russian functionaries.

Policy issues were related to shifting power in the Party rather than in worker interest or problems with difficulties with the regimes' practical impact on the economy. And to find policies which may in fact cause some economic improvements. So how bad do things need to get of be and what possibilities of policy are open short of central economic planning.

What level of frustration impacts the regime to move to more heavy handed actions? Is planning simply an ideologue symbol or rather is it the party apparatus which leads to insight into whether or central planning may in fact bring the results desire the way of economic change or provide only a superficial ideological plinth of leftist ideas—but which have little or no clarification of basic principles useful in directing an economy.

The use of economic planning gets written into economic history primarily because of the need for some type of economic organization in economies which impact the enduring economic crisis. For practical purposes that determines the power of political parties or political ideology. Does planning do what it was expected to do by the advisors and designers of the format? Not necessarily so - but rather to the impact on the political parties or regimes which favored the establishment of the planning system. Planning was means to strengthen or achieve national security. The types of planning were many and diverse. The differences reflected the institutional and political structure the political machinations and status that illustrated the socio-economic—political heritage of the different nations.

Planning initiatives took place in democracies and parliament and oligarchy systems. Some planning was indicative-that is implied, sent to the governing parties by the heads of State. The success of planning was and is a function of could be highly centralized or de-centralized power structures and with strong and less strong penalties for failure to comply with mandates and regulations by the state or planning bureaucracy.

The durability of planning models and structures was and continues to be tied not to the idea of planning or the form of planning or most important - not to the success of planning in ameliorating the economic crisis.

So starting after World War one, the Marxist ideologies were set up as a diversified area—with resources and a talented labor supply kind of ideological cloud hanging over an economy which was agricultural when there was need for increases in food and fiber and manufactured goods. There was period of ideological debates in1920-21 period in Russia. Names associated with ideas in the period were

Bukharin and Stalin. Issues were: Workers control of industry, the use of industrial trusts, and when should the state wither away. That was period which became known as "the end of utopianism." Bukharin was able put together something called "new economic policy" which alluded to Lenin's last ideas.in the thirties was a dominant economic issue for the USSR.

Debates continued for a period about issues raised by Stalin and Trotsky. Bukharin was a non-functionary. Incidentally Trotsky escaped to Mexico and was concerned with the direction of the Party and politicians and feared that there would be a shift of power away from farmers and factory workers to Party functionaries. A period when there was a struggle between the Party Left and Right. The right lost-Bukharin of the right was disposed and Stalin began his careful but slow movement to centralize his power in the party and/or the Left. The NEP lasted through most of 1920s. By 1927 Stalin had strengthen his position- Bukharin was a non-functionary. The trials and stabilization of the Stalin leftist regime.

The debates within the Party continued through the 1930s—with various reforms and structural administrative changes. Russia was still basically an undeveloped economy at the outbreak of WWII - with the aid of US Lend Lease Program skilled and talented labor force and huge agricultural areas for large grain supplies.

The war was carried out at high cost to the Russian. The settlements agreements between Roosevelt, Churchill and Stalin produced a new map of Europe and a sharp increase in the role of Russian economic connections with Europe. The Russians set up Communist Party control in newly acquired Balkan and Baltic areas. Russia got partial control--including state ownership, confiscation of property and assets. The regimes undertook a nationalization program with involved public transport, medical services, nationalization of companies and mines. The Communist Parties were under direct control of the Russian politicians. Economic and political decisions although vested in the local parties allowed for no deviation from the Russian edicts.

These annexed areas started its growing plans in a real sense in Russia after the move of the economy to the Left. Crisis of the government and the working through what resources and a talented labor supply was ----needed took the form of economic organization compatible with the Marxists/Leninist interpretation.

Dem Bones

Some technical stuff about economic central planning.

First, there has been a great revolution over the past two decades in the ability or capacity to manage or manipulate or replicate complex numerical or functional relationships. The progress could be tied to the increasing development of super computer systems.

So that means that a few installations around the world which may be able to handle the massive number of relationships that exist or could exist in an economic system. So now exists that is perhaps able to replicate enough economic processes to make central identification of factors, conditions, action of economic players and the structure of economic relationships identifiable and possibly manipulative enough to design or format economic relationships as variables in the economic functions or production and distribution of products as well as the relationships of inputs required in manufacturing, distribution and consumption actions or activities of an economy.

Think about economic activities as a large number of players making large number of decisions about buying, selling and consuming. Basically large number of institutions and relationships are designed and handled privately.

But back off a minute or two for different explanations. There was an old song which was somewhat popular many years ago. The song was "Dem Bones". Some of the lyrics were - the toes are connected to the footbone, the footbone is connected to the leg bone, the leg bone is connected to the knee bone, the knee bone is connected to the thigh bone and so on and on. Get it? There are connections, relationships and dependencies.

Good Old Days

The Old Days of "highly centralized" Governments.

Government programs in the former communist bloc countries, which for years, seemed to hold a fascination for liberals, included economic planning, nationalization of industry, and land collectivization programs. It is instructive to note the state or public ownership of resources seems to militate against effective market function even in countries where there is or was "democratic socialism."

According to the Economist, "western experience suggests that ownership is not what matters most in making markets work...A flourishing market requires competition, proper prices and proper incentives. But it would be wrong to conclude that who owns what is irrelevant." [see, "Privatizing Marx," The Economist, [Vol. 306,#7535] January 30, 1988, page 13.]

If there were no faulty markets, not even an ideal government or the best government economic policies can improve the efficiency with which resources are allocated. There are many, many circumstances where government has no advantage in information or transaction costs over the private market. It was argued that in the attempt to remedy market problems, the political processes and bureaucratic structure of a democratic society itself interferes with the proposed improvement. Even with the knowledge of market faults, there are logical reasons for relying on the existing market allocation processes.

In this second decade of the 21st Century,, there is no basis to assume that government programs designed to make markets function more effectively will or can do so, or reduce or solve economic problems.

But it seems that there is kind of widespread knowledge that to remedy market faults, "government" policies should be formulated and implemented. In the 1930s and again in the 1960s and 2000s, it was commonplace to identify a case of market in appropriation, and then conclude that government action was called for. If government programs failed, the fault was blamed on government bureaucrats. Legislative "follow up" and evaluation of the effectiveness or outcomes and effects of government programs might, if mandated by Congress, slow the pace of ineffective, costly, unsuccessful government programs.

The immediate response to the faulty appropriation processes of markets was to look for a solution to retain that best of all possible worlds. That was found in, of all places, government. Theorists then spent years and careers developing the exact prescriptions to give to government in order to correct perfectly for the ineffectiveness of the market.

Markets will fail and government interdiction will also fail as a reasonable approach to solve the problems.

But the pro-government advocates argue a "liberal approach" which implies that if government programs do not remedy the problem, it is better to continue the program rather than cut any government programs.

Market System - Need to Know

The information about market appropriation examples is very, very, important to the development of the information in many of the previous sections.

"Market" mechanisms are expected to facilitate product pricing, exchange, and the allocation of products, resources and income. There are apparently widespread "faulty market" problems in the economy.

There are many different types of cases of the capacity of markets to appropriate all of the needed data and information.

Faulty market appropriation refers to the extent of the markets' capacity to handle or include all economic allocation opportunities and decisions.

The term is a reference to the performance of the market mechanism, not the economic decision makers. Even under the best conditions, and if markets all function extremely well, markets will not function efficiently.

That sounds like a mistake or at least an inconsistency and paradox. But markets fail in the sense that markets do not and cannot provide adequate mechanisms to perform all of the allocation roles required.

The extent, cost and negative impact of the "market faults/appropriation" problems can be the basis for arguments that remedial policy intervention by the government is necessary.

Market faults appear because of less than optimum outcomes of the market, and because economic and political problems are created as a result of the policies designed to compensate for market inadequacies.

This information can be useful in understanding the extent to which various types of faulty markets affect our incomes and economic well-being, and our ability to be secure from manipulation by public and private institutions with extensive economic power.

The problems are the reasons for actions by policy makers to remedy the incidence and outcomes of market faults/appropriation. There are potential policies which may "do something about" the problems associated with real world market functions included later.

Did You Know?

A review pointed out non planning interest in careful creative programs. Issues related to population pressures and the environment and other issues whether the particular features of the proposals are workable, or can be implemented or have a basis in reality of possible outcomes consistent with needs as benefits to the general public benefactors.

Another Look at Planning Applications

A short conclusion about other nations using economic planning. Central government planning is not "the way to go" for most countries in the world. So why should the US - particularly the US and Obama - move to an economic control system that in and of itself is not functional as economic policy? The short answer is some version of leftist ideology and its related power to move the country to the left is the rational for Obama interest in central government planning.

The use of economic planning gets written into economic history primarily because of the need for some type of economic organization which impacts the enduring economic crisis. For practical purposes that determines the power of political parties or political ideology. Does planning do what it was expected to do by the advisors and designers of the format? Not necessarily so - but rather to the impact on the political parties or regimes which favored the establishment of the planning system. Planning was means to strengthen or achieve national security. The types of planning were many and diverse. The differences reflected the institutional and political structure the political machines nations and status that illustrated the socio-economic - political heritage of the different nations.

Planning initiatives took place in democracies and parliament and oligarchy systems. Some planning was indicative - that is implied - sent to the governing parties by the heads of State. The success of planning was and is a function of highly centralized or de-centralized power structures and with strong and less strong penalties for failure to comply with mandates and regulations by the state or planning bureaucracy.

The durability of planning models and structures was and continues to be tied not to the idea of planning or the form of planning or most important - not to the success of planning in ameliorating the economic crisis.

So starting after World War one, the Marxist ideologies was a set up as a diversified area—with resources and a talented labor supply - kind of ideological cloud hanging over an economy which was agricultural when there was need for increases in food and fiber and manufactured goods. There was period of ideological debates in the 1920-21 period in Russia. Names associated with ideas in the period were Bukharin and Stalin. Workers control of industry, use of industrial trusts, when should the state wither away. That was period which became known as "the end of utopianism." Bukharin was able put together something called "new economic policy" which alluded to Lenin's last ideas.in the thirties was a dominant economic issue for the USSR. Still in the category of an underdeveloped economy the challenges of development remain.

Debates continued for a period about issues raised by Stalin and Trotsky. Bukharin was a non-functionary. Incidentally

Bukharin Trotsky escaped to Mexico was concerned with the direction of the Party and politicians and feared that there would be a shift of power away from farmers and factory workers to Party functionaries. A period when there was a struggle between the Party Left and Right. The right lost- Bukharin of the right was disposed and Stalin began his careful but slow movement to centralize his power in the party and/or the Left. The NEP lasted through most of 1920s.

The debates within the Party continued through the 1930's with various reforms and structural administrative changes. Russia was still basically an undeveloped economy at the outbreak of WWII. With the aid of the US Lend Lease Program, a skilled and talented labor force and huge agricultural areas, large grain supplies were created. Hungary provided some wartime economic needs and were met by Russia using at the end of the war changed in maximum fashion the role of Russia European and World politics. The war was carried out at high cost to the Russians. The settlement agreements between Roosevelt, Churchill and Stalin produced a new map of Europe and a sharp increase in the role of Russian economic connections with Europe. The Russians set up Communist Party control in newly acquired Balkan and Baltic areas. Russia got partial control - including state ownership, confiscation of property and assets. The regimes undertook a nationalization program with involved public transport, medical services, nationalization of companies and mines. The Communist

Parties were under direct control of the Russian politicians. Economic and political decisions, although vested in the local parties, allowed for no deviation from the Russian edicts.

The war was won at high cost and sacrifice for Russians. Post recovery was aided by the distribution of countries between the West and the East. Russia acquired the Balkans, and Baltic countries and parts of Germany and control over parts of Austria. These annexed areas started its growing plans in a real sense in Russia after the move of the economy to the Left. Crisis of the government and the working through what resources and a talented labor supply was needed took the form of economic organization compatible with the Marxists/Leninist interpretation.

Post World War Two Impact

The satellite countries were integrated economically into the Soviet planning models. New sources of skilled labor and economic resources were adjuncts to the Russian resource base.

Poland added more seaborne connections with its ports. Poland provided a bureaucratic approach which was more practical administration and was followed with variations After WWII, the British Labour government situation in Russia. Slovakia became a region of heavy industrialization in the NW and SE. There were good agricultural lands in the central part of the country. Local regimes confiscated property and assets were state acquired. The planning system of the indicative type was favored by the Labour Party. There was nationalization of mines, transport, and companies. The designs used in the USSR engulfed the satellite countries. A model of prolonged debates in existed in eastern Europe. Yugoslavia's so-called World Council State was ended. Political dismemberment took precedent over the Tito approach to workers participation in national economic decisions.

Of course the Soviets ran the legal systems and controlled the press. The controlled court system was used to thin output and control any perceived threats to the regime.

During this period, eastern and southern European activity by the Reds were forays into state planning in other parts of

Europe. Forms of central planning spread through the economies of several States/s in the post-war two period.

Great Britain in a post war Recovery effort moved to the left fostered by the Labour Party. Britain moved back to the right under Thatcher.

Sweden turned to increase State controlled narrow short term projects than any other cases of Post War II examples. Sweden, Finland increased the government control after the War. It was identified as a "socialist state" with property nationalized and increased leftist institutional changes. The French planning was notably more successful in its use of bright, skilled approach more pragmatic approach and efforts. Germany and Italy were overtly pragmatic in designing economic policies which took maximum advantage of the cooperation with the West.

Background of Planning Uses

State planning was in use in Russia from the WWI through the next several decades. Russian planning interest as a durable issue involved many serious challenges to the interpretations of Lenin by Russian functionaries.

Policy issues were related to shifting power in the Party rather than in worker interest or problems with difficulties with the regimes' practical impact on the economy. And to find policies which may in fact cause some economic improvements. So how bad do things need to get of be and what possibilities of policy are open short of central economic planning.

Or what level of frustration impacts the regime to move more heavy handed action – whether or not planning is simply an ideologue symbol. Some were concerned that the party apparatus would lead to insight into whether central planning may in fact bring the results desired by way of economic change or provide only a superficial ideological plinth of leftist ideas - but which have little or no clarification of basic principles useful in directing an economy.

What Obama Will Do

Obama falls into the group of ideologues who suggest ideas without real interest or care whether a proposal can be carried effectively or may result in any effect other an increase in government largesse. Of course Obama will in the process be attentive to his political base of people who have no interest in ideology or any rational program development.

It is likely that Obama will continue his search for incremental leftist programs. That means a push or direction to set up some organization for economic planning. It may be the decentralized type or what is called indicative planning. It will be without complete state ownership of resources. The move to administering the economy ---not to make the economic reform from the recession operative--- but to fulfill ideological precepts based on some unidentified ideology.

*The availability of management of huge amounts of data and strong support from the media would suggest that the leftist bent is in place and easy to manipulate in the short run. This is another case of a presidential political move to support a program or economic policy which no one wants or would support - but another case of policy failure without rational support or testing - a bad and destructive move by the administ*ration.

This type of planning is directive, without heavy administrative control, usually referred to as "indicative" planning. Indicative planning provides macro outcome goals, and with some government influence from fiscal and monetary policy, and should permit the private sector market forces to determine allocation and distribution in the economy. This type of planning differs from the command type which requires that government decision makers control allocation and distribution decisions and activities.

Other nations employing the socialist elements of state ownership or nationalized industries and with non-democratic, one party political system had different structures and mechanisms for economic organization.

Numerous Latin American countries have state ownership of some industries, but no planning and questionable political democracies and/or dictators.

The decentralization meant that the central government could not allocate economic resources between de-centralized republics. The de-centralized structure changed from forms of worker management to contractual arrangements between groups of workers. These contracts determined the type of services that each labor group would provide. Many enterprise decisions were in fact controlled by these worker group contract arrangements.

Banking was also decentralized but funds could not be transferred through the banking system from one republic to another. The central government was virtually stripped of its influence on the republic's outlays for development programs. The republics were practically financially independent. Funds could be moved from the republics to the

Federal government only for social security and defense programs. The federal government could not allocate the republics' funds for programs which would equalize incomes, or to create employment opportunities or for economic and growth programs.

At the beginning of the 1990s, de-centralization was on-going. There were more reforms in the political pipeline which would have permitted market demand and supply to determine and dominate economic activity and relationships. The means to bring privatization of most enterprises were also being designed. The Yugoslav economy at the end of the 1980s was the most economically de-centralized of any of the former "communist" economies and most republics looked to the ultimate economic decentralization that the "market economy" would provide.

The key term here is opening—state controls on the economy were substantially removed which permitted the emergence of the energy of Indian entrepreneurs. An export focus and more "outward oriented" development orientation by the government facilitated a shift in resources to the private sector. The public finances were shaped to no longer to be a drag on the private sector. Those reforms have permitted India to achieve real growth rates of over 6 percent per year to emerge as a major player in the world economies.

But China followed the Soviet central, command-planning model until the 1960s. China then discovered that it was disadvantaged in its adoption of the Soviet type industry-first model because it was "labor long" and "land and resources short."

In fact, the China case confirmed that only the economies which are very rich in resource endowment could emulate the Soviet style central economic planning. Also as in the former Soviet Union in the early stages of its industrialization, Chinese industry development was underway.

There has been pragmatism at work in the administration of economic change in China. In fact the system can be called, "pragmatic socialism." Some regions and industries operate almost of a free market like basis, while other industries and regions are under greater central control. The Chinese government relied on "industry development policy" to direct investment and financial resources for the production of specific products in specific areas of the country.

The Communist East Bloc countries continued until the 1990's under the influence of the Soviet authorities. Centralized planning abounded but with some local country differences. The former German Democratic Republic was an effective imitator of the Soviet style central planning model. Bulgaria was a close second to East Germany in the central control of the economy.

But Romania followed a modified central planning model based on the ideas of a strong despotic leader. Albania was the worst case example of the ineffectiveness of centralized planning in resource short economies. Hungary, until the radical reforms in the late 1980s, was characterized by an atypical form of state ownership and macroeconomic planning. Demand and supply was permitted to influence economic activity at the retail market level. Prior to the great economic upheavals in the East Block, Hungary and Slovakia had been a leader in establishing joint ventures with capitalist economies. Of course after the moves to democracy and to market oriented economies, all of the former Soviet satellites increased economic relations of all types with the West.

Paths to Change

In the decades just prior to the 21st Century, the vector of decreased central government economic control was in play in almost all of the "socialist and communist" nations. Short of moving to a market allocation system, the types of reforms needed in state controlled economies were quite clear. There were enough "on the ground" cases of failed economic allocation to provide a plinth of knowledge to direct the process and structure of reforms.

It was likely that increased unemployment, higher prices and shortages could accompany any major reforms. But the necessary, tough reforms needed to include price reforms to make prices reflect "real costs." Real or meaningful incentives were needed at enterprise levels. Enterprises needed to be able to determine their capital investment needs. The enterprise profits should be based on real performance. Real incentives, not propaganda, were needed for labor.

Demand in consumer goods markets should be transmitted to producers. That would mean an end to the success criterion of "volume of output sold". Comparative advantage should be permitted to play a role in international trade patterns. That would mean the end of the state monopoly of trade decisions.

Market-like capital allocation should determine money allocation.

Such reforms moved the economies, making the reforms, closer to a market type economy. The market economy type reforms held promise of both short term problems and longer terms improvements for many of the former socialist or planned economies.

More on Planning

Even today you can see evidence of central planning in East Europe - a legacy of the Soviet planning efforts. If you drive from Slovakia to Poland, A careful observer of the countryside, you would be quick to notice the road and highway system. In Slovakia there is little evidence of "farm to market roads." But in Poland you will see in contrast, a pattern of access to local economic intuitions or the presence of "farm to market roads." So? Well in Slovakia, farm workers were living and employed on community estates collective activity. At harvest time, there was no need for local farmers about getting their products to markets. There were no real vehicular arrangements. Transportation was by truck or bus. Resources and supplies necessary for the farm had collective identification not personal. In Poland the level of collectivization was different, perhaps as a result of some influence of the church. Anyway private vehicles were available and could be contracted out for needs by the worker groups. The roll of the church in Poland is a different topic and reserve for a look at another time. Re: the church - another case - In Hungary. There is evidence that, in earlier times, under the Nazi - that the export of Jews from Hungary to the death camps was delayed and later than in the other East Block. There are heroes of this era for your view and study in Budapest. This is trivia in terms of economic processes but extremely important to the human condition.

Shift Here - Now Comes "Ethics"

Even if selective reforms reduce corporate concentration and the excess profit source of economic power, economic disparity will not end. Even if corporate economic power were decentralized and markets were more "competitive," problems of the low income poor will persist.

The syndrome of causes of poverty includes: high prices for needed consumer goods, bad supervision in bad jobs, limited upward mobility in part-time minimum wage jobs, bad labor market information, and the lack of access to high productivity job options.

It is not worthwhile to argue that corporations, per se, are responsible for causing secular poverty, but it is productive to identify the connection between the corporation and the spiritually poor rich.

A differentiation between the secularly poor and the spiritually poor, and the spiritually poor rich, helps to differentiate corporate responsibility.

There is a basis for linking the rich who are possessed by their possessions with a corporate ethos. Unrelenting devotion to amassing possessions through higher income is a common attribute of the "professionals" in corporations. It is the commitment to materialism which is a "corporate cause of spiritual poverty." The remedy for spiritual poverty, whether for the high or low income persons, is the purge of their materialistic proclivities. No effective remedy can be administered by any external secular agency. Any remedy

60

must be sourced to a personal commitment to overcome the persuasiveness of materialistic acquisitions and egocentrism of position or personal aggrandizement.

The spiritually poor-rich could affirm a commitment to unselfishness and to being a blessing to others. The individual as a Christian has the obligation to be humble and is mandated by biblical imperatives to be a steward and foregoer.

Foregoer activities of the rich are essential to redistribute economic power away from the corporation. But those richer rich must not become more or remain spiritually poor. The Biblical warnings about not being possessed by possessions apply - of course, to those rich and to all of us. God expects the rich to be effective stewards who are well directed in foregoing their own use of their resources—by redistributing wealth to the poor.

The topic is business responsibility - How does that work? Who does what?

Legislative Intervention - Financial Reform

About legislative changes that may show elements of the pattern of the current ideology of an enhanced government role to amend and remedy some of the issues related to "market failures and market faults." The pattern of legislative actions focused on regulatory devices to assure that government interjection in private sector decision making is feature of the near term future.

Start with the much heralded financial regulatory "reform."

The near-collapse of the world financial system in the fall of 2008 and the global credit crisis that followed gave rise to widespread calls for changes in the regulatory system. A year and a half later, Congress passed a bill expanding the federal government's role in the markets, reflecting a renewed mistrust of financial markets after decades in which Washington stood back from Wall Street with wide-eyed admiration.

In a general way the legislation reflects the influence of the President's views announced the summer of 2009 resembled the sweeping reform legislation President Obama had proposed in June 2009. Its progress was marked by fierce industry lobbying and partisan battles, as almost all Republicans voted against the measure -- battles likely to continue as regulators hash out the many large questions left unresolved by the legislation.

The House of Representatives passed a version of a bill in December 2009. Then In May 2010, the Senate side passed a generally similar bill. In the Senate, there were three Republican Senators—Snowe, Collins of Maine and Brown voted in favor of the bill. One Democrat, Feingold of Wisconsin, opposed the legislation.

The framers and supporters of the legislation argued that the legislation ended more than a generation when the general view toward the financial industry was "one of hands-off" resulting in deregulation. Supporters of the legislation assert that the legislation does not match the tough restrictions put in place at the time of the 1930's depression. Supporters also argued that there is a new distrust of the financials plus uncertainty about the increasing complexity and complexity of the role of technology in the markets, pushed the need for some relief and protection of the average American.

What the legislation is supposed to bring about is an expansion of regulation over banks and public markets. That includes expanded oversight of a wider range of financial companies and putting into play regulation of the huge volume of trading in credit derivatives.

A "council of federal regulators," was set up to be chaired by led by the Secretary of the Treasury. The regulators are charged with the, coordination of revelations about risks to the financial system. The legislation may give certain revelations restrict and/or close the companies involved.

There is also a new and seemingly powerful "regulator", to be housed at the Federal Reserve, and, chosen by the President. That regulator is charged with the protection of consumers and of financial products." It is likely that there will be a two year lapse before activity by the regular is apparent in a simplified "disclosure for mortgage loans."

Levitt has provided a review of the legislation with these comments,. Levitt's opinion was published in the Wall Street Journal, [06/24/2010, page A19]. " . . . I had hoped the financial reform bill would be the best example of my party's long standing reputation for standing on the side of individual investors. It's not." . . . "The Democrats had the chance to do this bill the right way. They should have been motivated by Congress's previous failure to adopt meaningful reform, which left investors unprepared for the crisis."

Levitt pointed pout several issues that he has with the approach in the legislation: One: Public companies will now have a wider loophole to avoid doing internal audits investors can trust." But the reform bill expands the number of small companies exempt from Sarbanes-Oxley audit requirements. Two: Congress failed to revoke the 1975 law that prevents municipal bond issuer from facing the kind of regulation and scrutiny of the corporate bond market. Three: they failed to pass a meaningful majority-vote or proxy access rule for corporate ballots. . . . And the Democratic leadership left in place the confusing dual regulatory structure of the SEC and the Commodity Trading

Commission. More: the bill failed to support a new law to overcome the legal precedent which allows third party consultants, accountant and other abettors of fraud to avoid liabilities. And one more: Congress did not deal with the massive problems of Fannie Mae and Freddie Mac.

Economic Policy Effects

The effects of government spending may or may not be identifiable, even for people in the smart group. That conclusion should certainly give rise to your concern about being smart about the effectiveness, timing, and composition of federal government expenditure policies and programs.

Probably the most important of the known economic effects stem from the fact that expenditures have exceeded revenues for years.

When expenditures are larger than revenues, the government "borrows" from the private sector to make up the revenue needs. The amount borrowed in a fiscal year is called the annual deficit. If the annual deficit is not retired or paid off, it is added to prior annual deficits. The cumulative total of the annual deficits is called the "national debt." Since the early 1990's, annual deficits were running at about $150 billion and the accumulated total national debt was well over $3 trillion. In the 2000s, the annual deficits and the total national debt ballooned and Increased at an increasing rate. If you compare the debt to economy's output of goods and services [GDP], that percentage was about 350 percent. Kind of like it was in the 1930s, and a 100 point increase 1997 to 2007.

In the summer of 2010, there had been a Congressional Budget Office reporting of a $4.4 trillion added since 2008. The annual deficit in 2010 was about $1.4 trillion and the total debt was over $13.5 trillion. The national debt has continued to increase and average of $4.11 billion per day since September 28, 2007. On a per capital basis, the share for each person is about $44,000.

The pattern of deficit spending with annual deficits is the current rule rather than the exception. Those dollar amounts seem large-they are large. There is no way for the average person to visualize the physical size of a trillion or so dollar debt.

It sounds like big numbers. Is it too big?

How can you tell if the deficits are too large?

But first, it may make sense to add on a bit more about what the debt is and how the government goes about creating the public debt.

Doing Government Debt

What does the "debt" look like? Where is it? Who has it? Do you owe any money to the government? Is the debt a problem?

If you want to see what the largest portion of the debt looks like, you can get a list of what makes up the debt by looking at the financial page of a national or good local newspaper. In the sections where stock market and commodity reports appear is a small section on government finance. There are usually a couple of columns listing numbers for different types of debt instruments. The listing shows the bid and asked prices, the change from the day before, the maturity date and the estimated yield.

The types include bills, notes and bonds. These names identify different types of debt instruments. These instruments arc not new issues but are already in a secondary market. These are types of IOUs or promises to pay issued by the government. The different types vary by length of maturity and the interest paid by the government to the owners. The bills are short term with three months, or six months and one year maturity. Notes typically mature in two years or up to five or seven years. Bonds are longer term with maturities from seven or more years up to thirty years. The Treasury changes the maturities to fit the conditions that are understood to be operational in the money markets. The Treasury attempts to be flexible about the structure of the debt and the debt instruments.

The interest yield that the government pays to debt owners—on the long bonds may be higher than on the shorter maturity bills and notes.

But the note and bond rates may be quite close. The interest yield to buyers and thus the interest cost to the government is basically determined by the supply and demand conditions in the huge or open money and capital markets.

Treasury securities of whatever type are very safe since they are backed by the "full faith and credit" of the U.S. government. There is virtually no risk of default to the owners of these instruments and the yields are a reflection of market changes in the interest rates. These debt instruments are "as good as you can get" in terms of risk aversion. The federal government has never defaulted on its debt, at least in the last several hundred years.

The securities are easy to sell and buy-they are marketable! There is a ready secondary market for the purchase or sale of the debt instruments. So these debt instruments and government securities are attractive "investments" for persons, and public and private, domestic and foreign institutions.

No one is quite sure who the buyers and owners of government marketable securities are. Note the term, "marketable"—describes the types of securities listed above. But there is non-marketable debt issued as well—in the form of "savings bonds." Savings bonds are issued by agents of the Treasury usually local depository institutions. These bonds have a stated interest rate and a stated maturity date. Maturities keep being shortened in order to raise the effective interest rate. These bonds cannot be bought and sold in the money or capital markets, but must be redeemed or cashed at an agency of the Treasury. The bonds are also issued in the name of the bearer, so ownership is by registration.

In the case of the marketable securities, ownership is by possession. In the case of the non-marketable bonds, persons can actually see and hold them as interest earning securities. But with the non-marketable instruments possession is not possible, or not needed for that matter. In most cases the owner or ownership is listed on a computer record and the debt instrument is not even printed.

Marketing Debt

It is apparent that people or agencies and institutions willingly buy and hold the government debt. The government type IOUs are interest earning assets.

Nobody except depository institutions is required to buy or own government debt.

The Fed in its open market activity may cause financial institutions to get out of excess reserves and into government securities to limit create expansion. So banks and other depository institutions are big owners of debt. Universities, pension funds, corporations, foundations, churches, and U.S. government agencies, and foreigners and governments, and foreign banks purchase and hold government debt. Some of our government debt is denominated in foreign currency units to make it easy for foreigners to buy our debt. The U.S. Treasury has been active in encouraging foreign purchases of the debt. There are thousands of billions of dollars of U.S. debt in the hand of foreigners. As you would assume, China is the foreign biggest buyer of U.S. debt.

It has been estimated that persons own only between 10 and 20 percent of all the marketable securities. So unless you made arrangements to buy government debt, you do not own any. And be assured, there is no massive file in Washington with your name in it indicating how much of the government you owe.

Once more—there is no massive file in Washington with your name in it indicating how much of the government you owe. The journalistic ideas about every man, woman and child in the country owing so many dollars of the national are just metaphors and are basically silly.

"It is the Media that is Ignorant!"

So how do you buy government debt when you want to? Most government debt is not sold directly by the Treasury or government. The Federal Reserve is largely responsible for handling government debt instruments. An individual or any buyer can go to a Fed Res bank on designated days of the weeks and submit a "bid" on specific debt instrument to be issued. So buyers with at least $10,000 can bid for the new bill issues at the Fed. The bills are issued to be sold in $5,000 multiples above the $10,000 minimum. Five year notes and longer term issues are available in multiples of $1,000, with the minimum of $1,000.

There are about 40 or so large commercial and investment banks which are called primary dealers. They are in a rather exclusive club authorized by the Federal Reserve Bank of New York to trade directly with the Federal Reserve. This is an active "club." New three months and six months bills are sold every week. The Treasury sells one year bills every four weeks. The three year and 10 year notes and 30 year bonds are typically sold once each quarter.

The primary dealers submit bids for the new issues. On the basis of a successful bid, a primary dealer buys the debt from the Fed and in turn makes the market for the disposition. The primary dealer knows the clientele of ready and willing buyers. The dealers make profit on the volume, tied to the spread between its purchase price and the resale price.

Traders are aggressive and individual traders can try to "corner the market" on particular issues.

The Treasury releases information on the new issues about five days in advance of the sale. Financial dealers and their customers begin trading the securities, and guessing on the actual sale price. This advance trading helps the primary dealers to estimate the "demand" for the new issues. Buyers do not have to deal with dealers, and may buy directly from the Federal Reserve.

Any Connection Between Debt and Money?

The buying and selling of federal debt instruments has direct and indirect impacts in the money markets. Who buys the debt and how the debt is paid for are important determinants of the impact of the federal security market activities.

For example, if the new government securities are purchased by banks. The buyers would be either commercial or the Federal Reserve banks. When banks buy, they make payment to the Treasury and that would reduce the banks' reserves at the Fed. There is, however, no effect on the money supply, because there is only a switch of funds, not the creation of new money. But when the Treasury begins to spend this increase in their deposits by writing checks, the additional deposits show up in the banks' total reserves and the money supply is increased. In a hypothetical case, if the Federal Reserve were to buy new government debt, which it does not does, neither the money supply nor bank reserves would change, but the money supply would change when the money is spent by the government. The Fed is not.

Modernity in Planning

You now know something about central government planning.

Consumers and consumer goods were low priority and found product lines limited and poorly designed. When in the WWII period, the Russians drove the Nazi out of east Europe, Property was transferred to the State. Production priorities favored heavy industry and agriculture. Travel was restricted and the job market was Party controlled. Party members held top jobs and a Party member ship was necessary for education jobs Consumers and consumer goods were low priority and found product lines limited and portly designed.

In the modern era, the shift to the availability and capacity of super computers would see to permit an incremental improvement in the handling of large masses of economic data. IT is clear that the IRS, NSA, and other government agencies can and do process, accumulate and manipulate a huge volume of data. And some US government agencies have doing this for years.

Now it would seem that it might be feasible for the government to set into place the hundreds of thousands of inter relationships in the economic processes which a are part of every life and times of our economy.

It can be assumed that the Obama Administration knew this when it put together the Obama Health Care plan. It is important to note that processes required to manage by government of about 16-19 percent of the economy - the health care dimensions - could be managed by educators and technicians familiar with high capacity computers. Some examples such as in France, the extent of the coverage of economic control was limited to infrastructure and to urban project development projects. Some examples such as in France, the extent of the coverage of economic control was limited to infrastructure and to urban project development projects.

Planning Is a Type of Economic Control System - Got It?

To have effective economic planning of industrial production and distribution, there must be unusual types of controls to assure that each planned activity is workable and practical through a series of steps in the production, distribution and allocation process.

Planning is basically an alternative to the independent decisions made in an enterprise- capitalistic system.

Economic system planning provides a government bureaucratic agency to make the decisions about economic tasks and processes

In the planned economic systems, the administration of factor and product markets has been legitimized by fiat, law or encompassment to have public employees used as the primary decision maker. In such a system, there can be traditional economic mal-functions   Entrepreneurship has been excluded. . The presence of deviation from the planned functions show up in the form of recession, depression, high unemployment, low incomes, etc. Such conditions are not supposed to appear in a recession, a depression or economic chaos.

Devolution—that is flexibility--- from the centralized types of decisions— is not permitted or tolerated. The appearance of system impairment processes was/is the most inactivating factor in or of planned economic allocation and distribution.

.

The impact on such persons who might be accused of deviation is to do whatever might seem effective in getting the system back to a condition prior to the problems. Failure to find effective remedy falls on plan administrators not the plan itself.

Persons involved or accused may be removed from the job, removed from the Party. Short term problems or exigencies were managed using a technique called "beg, borrow or steal"

Serious managerial failures were managed by removal from the Party roles and then to prison or shooting of petty bureaucrats.

In large scale projects such as in USSR—there was a huge bureaucracy, with thousands of people in the labor force working on plans and the structure of the planning agencies constituted an organizational bottleneck and management problem in and of itself. You can trace through a litany of sequences where a bottleneck could appear in transmitting micro level orders to the people on the work force where the Russians had established their typical planning system and priorities. Since there was no private ownership, all/any property was the element of production or distribution. Such large scale planning functions could not be expected to feature flexibility in organization, or frequent design of products, or style changes etc. Routine, stability and no interruption were the features of nationwide central planning.

Little priority was paid to innovation per se or product design or new product availability.

Other planning examples such as in post war France, - the extent of the coverage of economic control was limited to infrastructure and to urban development projects. This case is not decentralized as such, but is pared down. The number of decisions is smaller. The impact of the planning processes was not distributed throughout the economy. And management functions are easier to fill. In the case of France-there were relatively few planners on the projects. Most of the planners were academics at several universities. And the success of the projects was physical and economic development—not the enhancement of political parties. Consumers and consumer goods were low priority and found product lines limited and poorly designed.

The Russian occupiers set up their traditional planned economic system - in Slovakia, East Germany, etc.

Property was transferred to the State. Production priorities favored heavy industry and agriculture. Travel was restricted and the job market was Party controlled. Party members held top jobs and a Party member ship was necessary for education jobs. Almost all college professors were members of the Communist party.

Incidentally the Reds also controlled religion. The Communists placed all local pastors and church officials on the State payrolls. Service on Sunday was permitted but there could be no membership drive activity. There was a list "of acceptable hymns and sermon topics" that pastor could use. Vitiations could mean job removal or in a few cases, pastors were removed to prison. Control of religion was a sub set of Party control.

If you were caught in a snow storm in Budapest and needed a pair of boots. Boots were sold in a state store but a few stores did carry footwear. If you found a store which sold footwear you would find one style and be lucky if here was a size distribution that you wanted.

Also in the WWII period of Russian occupation of East Europe, large numbers of Russians in the military were moved to Slovakia—including their families. These were the elitists and Party members.

Another example—if a Party member had car trouble—a few did use cars—the car would be dropped off at a repair center. The Party member would go in the shop and simply tell the workers to stop what you are doing and fix my car. So there were class dis along with Party members got priority housing and services. There were many stories of Russian behavior during the period—including one about clothing choice and availability for women.

Slovak's used to snicker when they would see Russian women show up in restaurants or concerts in slips, night gowns and panties. Those types of clothes, attractive to Russian women, had been available at home in Russia but not available in stores in Russia at the time.

The Communist Party members were elitists in the classless society. They got priority over the average worker or consumer. Incidentally the pay scale for workers was the same throughout the economies - Russia, also in the East Block. Income in money and real goods were first allocated to Party members.

When in the WWII period, the Russians drove the Nazi out of east Europe,   Property was transferred to the State. Production priorities favored heavy industry and agriculture. Travel was restricted and the job market was Party controlled. Party members held top jobs and a Party member ship was necessary for education jobs.

Almost all college professors were members of the Communist party Incidentally the Reds also controlled religion. The Communists placed all local pastors and church officials on the State payrolls. Services on Sunday were permitted but there could be no membership drive activity. There was a list "of acceptable hymns and sermon topics that pastor could use. Violations could mean job removal or in a few cases, pastors were removed to prison. Control of religion was a subset of Party control.

Now Think About This

This is a kind of outline or symbolic structure of what is in the pages in this book.

Points to know:

1. The Obama regency government is leftist;

2. The left leaning public policy has the integral feature of socialist government roles in economics;

3. The socialists' orientation includes control of all economic activities in the US;

4. The economic structure for a leftist economy is government control or elimination of the current widespread functioning of private decision making in a private sector with a leadership role being played by business owners, entrepreneurs and consumers;

5. The ultimate goal for socialists to achieve economic methods of control is to use "economic planning" centralized at the federal level;

6. Economic planning is not new has a rich history of failures and lack of successes in remedying economic problems;

7. Efforts to resolve economic problems such as a recession, depressions, unemployment, slow growth and income distribution are supposed to be subject to a pattern of government policies, planning which are assumed by Socialists to be remedial.

8. The mechanics of obtaining adequate and timely planning inroads to solve particular issues such as unemployment and assumed inequities in income distribution.

How does planning get established in an economy?

By the vote of the electorate, military action, usurpation of existing economic processes because of the effectiveness of government of charismatic political leaders, higher taxes, increases in business regulation, government standards, for private sector businesses, programed about the largess of government programs under expanded social control, government sponsored lying about and so on increased the previous point if applied to the US economy might assume that political leadership devised and defined for a political leaders with propaganda support from an organized communication hierarch is the America case.

9. But where are we in the US or what evidence is apparent that the Obama socialists are trying to use or insert central government planning to transform the obvious problems off low economic performance?

10. There are two areas that suggest that the Obama Administration is in a long process of wanting to advance the use of economic planning. The major indicators are the politicization of information gathering by NSA and the use of the IRS in enforcement of forced payments included in the Obama health program. And efforts to install a single payer structure of medical care.

What is the real NSA role and connection? In prior cases of central planning of large industrial societies are the numerical relationships or coefficients of connection between production, distribution and or consumption of goods and services.

The major process difficulty has been the adequacy and availability of data and the technical capacity to create and make available the connections or consecutive relationships between and within the round abruptness of industrial and economic processes."

Recall "Dem Bones?"

Maybe a diversion here?

Remember the old popular ditty - "dem bones"? The connectedness in the human relationships indicates linkages that are in place to have the body do its activities and functions. With a bit of a stretch supposed you looked an economic process of cattle farming. Take the case of feed for farm animals. Cattle require to be fed to cause growth which will produce an adequate quality of beef for consumption. Or how much of what feed is needed per head of cattle to facilitate growth adequate to result in marketable beef? So look at the number and type of functions involved. Feed comes from agriculture commitment of land use to make the basic ingredient of cattle food. How much farm land should be allocated by planners to assure adequate acreage is available. How much mechanical equipment is needed to assure that seed planting, cultivation during growth, and how much equipment should be produced to assure harvesting can be adequate? Or how many spare parts for what type of equipment needs to be reproduced to assure repairs can be timely. How is the completed feed to be transported? WHAT RESOURCES DO THE RAILROADS NEED TO ASSURE THAT TRANSPORT WILL BE ADEQUATE?

Go on - back to the growing farm site - how much fertilizer of what kinds are needed to assure adequate growth from the land resource. How much fuel of what types should be planned to planting, growing and harvesting?

No need to go on with this jungle of relationship example.'

To be sure there is massive need for data and a functional relation or relationships to handle what the planners must know in order to make basic plans and to monitor production or distribution in process.

Until the epic of the massive or super computer, no central planning system ever was able to get the coefficients between products, products lines, transfer data from one industry sector to another or a complete picture of the coefficients in all economic processes for planning purposes.

The super computer capacity has been illustrated in the Snowden situation. It seems that the government now has the means and capacity and availability to record and process billions of pieces of economic data that could be manipulated by computer technicians to develop a system of relationships in the economic functions to make if feasible to provide the Socialist planner with the information that is needed to make central planning work!!!!

The degree of difficulties inherent in the structure of the Obama care legislation could be used as a further example of the leftward to control and centralized decision making in the current regime.

Be careful now in trying to make that system of a single planner or planners agency that would be used to control the other 80 percent of the economy per se.

The Obama care legislation is in and of itself a bureau valuating the management of massive economic information for an interim stage of moving directly from single payer to another structure which has been added to government roles in the last decade.

The computer system hang-ups that took place were attributed by some critics as an ineffective design of access means and devices. What the home page and registration via computer were in fact the testing of a system to have a series of ways to move to assure control of about 18 percent of so of economic activity in the US economy. The period of failure of access was a trial period.

That is what is important here.

The one term is the word "Uncertainty"

In previous pages, people who focused on ethics and private inference and intrusion were described as just muddling around with no real position or uniformed opposition to the Obama administration. It is like the adage that applies to the stock market - you have to move the money. The clever and creative options have been moved   in an inexorable way for the left.

Timing, mandates, substantive concepts and other diversionary programs have popped up in the steady style as if the durability of the quality of other issues is not important.

What is important for Obama is to keep changing the topic or focus while the economic and political ventures of the Administration go on unabated?

Looking to the future pattern of change is problematical for the regime. Timing may be an issue. There has been coverage of the idea of the Obama legacy that he wanted conserved regardless of the how the changes are managed or put to effect.

Who is it or what groups support the concept of an Obama legacy?

Or what ideology is the source of the structural and programmed changes in the legacy?

What happened is that the advocates of increasing centralization have moved only some public support for inclusion in a legacy.

What is included or showed up on a lot of pages in this volume? These overviews and historical perspectives should have been adequate for you to understand that you must recognize the symbolism of Snowden.

There is no evidence that it is hard to find any use or advantage to this form of economic organizations. The form and structure of modern economic or state planning has benefited immensely from the use of the massive or giant computer.

With no concern about ethics the old mechanical constraints in getting and managing the thousands of variables and their relationships has been what Obama wants to be in his legacy.

The reviews in the previous sections concluded that were various options and techniques that may come into play to assure that Obama legacy does in fact exists for the future.

It is not clear which of the techniques or tools will be put into place or by whom or when?

In one area, there is less uncertainty - and that is the overriding pressure for pushing programs and techniques to the left.

-That left push is axiomatic. Obama's thrusts for change will not allow any programs or activities that might allow intrusions of such computers rationality.

Only passing symbolic concerns about what the government needs to know and how will any information is used.

But there are techniques available to the left to sidetrack ethical and judicial concerns.

There is evidence that Obama **MIGHT CAUSE ANY RECOGNITION OF THE POSSIBILITIES OF TRYING TO USE THE MARKET MECHANISM** *as source or direction for positive changes for the private sector.*

State in Economic Decision Making

However ethical and ideological reservations reduce the list of certainties as central economic control. The usual form of that control is through the concept application of "central government economic planning."

Central government economic planning no longer faces the physical and mechanical constraints that plagued older uses of planning.

The modern massive, high speed processors are one major permissive factor in urging leftist ideologues to resurrect or revitalize central government planning. It is logical for the left to want to move to more central government control of the economy. The means and method to do that is the wave of the future for leftist like Obama. Such planning may be a vital feature of the Obama legacy.

Start of the End

Obama indicated that he would use executive orders and his pen to get what he wanted - from a Congress which he viewed as unproductive. The great bill stopping machining in the Congress over the past several years was the work of Harry Reid. Reid may be gone in the nearer future. Check the numbers - and the Republicans never figured a socio-political approach that permitted them from being labeled as impotent.

To "fix" or make operational the Obama health care structure and administration will mean the end of traditional role of private sector insurance companies. Evidence suggests that the goal of the Administration is to dissolve the private insurance sector to be replaced by the government single payer device. There has been little evaluation of what the demise of the rational private insurance companies will mean to the general economy.

The country may be faced with another Obama law change-even more heavy handed than the Obama care mandate changes in 2013 and 2014.

With elimination of the private sector via the single payer/mandates, The insurance companies may also opt to buy government debt as an investment into the system as business or personal investment flows.

It is not clear what steps could be taken by whom to prevent or invalidate such a move. No one seemed to know what to do about the arbitrary date changes that made in the mandates in 2013 and 2014.

A lot depends on the media and what it tries to convey to the ignorant and ill-informed about a justification for the extension of the Obama legacy.

No hope from the media in slowing down the pell mell rush to push the country further to the left.

To continue with your worrying:

Heavy duty future worries are related to the future of the economy.

Since 2008 the economy has not prospered. Economic policies The Administration need to be able to shut off or down and more revelations about behavioral activities. Some of that information may be additions to the Administration's extensive interference with the kind of individual freedom that most Americans favor and treasure.

That included fabrication of the program, outright lying by the Democratic Party spokes' people and creating a veil of ignorance which preventing people from finding what was in the legislation.

You never hear of anything about policies to strengthen the market system.

A more centralized non market system is what the Obama regime will opt for.

The more leftward tilt is likely to be what Obama wants to be preserved as his legacy. Prognosticators assume that a larger more complete role of the federal government will be necessary - by default and in action.

What was included in the pages in this small book was a look at knowledge about the background and the effectiveness of policies based on the market as well as the evaluation of the mirages and actual impacts of central government economic planning.

Toward Central Planning

The fatal inexorability of the Obama design to use new found technology to set up central planning is the most and important political and economic issue facing the US economic system.

There are a number of permissive factors, programs, legislation and support for transforming the current US economy into a system that will no longer be private enterprise capitalism, but some as yet unknown and untested centrally control system

A related issue is 'who cares'?

Who has this expectation of change and what if anything can be done to side track the Obama leftist juggernaut to centralization and loss of a workable structure of the economy.

Remember that Obama care is the test case, now in place as to the feasibility of overcoming previous technical barriers of organization data procurement and management. If there is no recognition of the Obama thrusts obviously nothing is now being undertaken to thwart the incursions.

And there are few people in the economy, likely to create a response of interference to stop the insurgency. Remember that Obama has indicated that he can bypass the legislative branch to get programs in place that he has favored.

His comments about having a pen and cell phone is all that he needs to make changes in income distribution. So as a practical matter is it likely that the House and Senate would have no functional role in the transformation and transition. The legislative branch has had its independence neutralized and would to a failed vehicle of the political type to slow the push to central planning.

Media and most news figures are not equipped to analyze what the administration does or wants to do.

Conservation talk radio personalities by default focus of minutia of public policy and may struggle to get any significant or persistent public acknowledgement of the perils on the horizon.

It may well be that at some time in the future that there will be a military recognition and act as leadership in activities which for functional purposes will be too late. And with or without military support there is no tradition in the United States for action by the military or public in the form of uprisings and street protests.

The Republican political party continues to illustrate ineptness and the loss of focus on the internal integrity of the party.

The general public must develop support against the battering of the Constitution and the planning umbrella. But since the topic and magnitude of change is so new, it would be fool hearty to write off the role of individuals in descent and or embracing public opposition to the planning move.

Of course the judicial system has or should have a role in arbitrary judgment calls by the executive branch.

Been swinging left and picking precedent cases for public decision making to suggest that the judicial is a lagging indicator of forces necessary to slow the move to central planning.

So is it a lost cause to try to construct opposition to the Obama inroads on the Presidency. There is no reason assume that he will be removed from Presidential politics or other politics. His role cannot be forecast with any certainty. It would be like extrapolation of search for new political power in the United States.

But the entrails of his regime will be inherited by someone in some version of the former the Democratic Party - and also with the yet to be former politicians who will tag along in their typical non-thinking manner to continue the vestiges of the failed Obama machine. And it may be that the next Democratic Party candidate will simply follow the substance and directions of the Obama regime.

But the time remaining for his regime is an ongoing uncertainty closing of opportunities available to move quick enough to implement the highest level of economic control.

BUT WAIT - OF THE SITUATIONS THAT WERE POINTED OUT AS PERMISSIVE FACTOR IN OTHER SECTIONS.

THE USE OF THE MODERN LARGE SCALE COMPUTERS will be central government planning system and other ways of getting data of the type needed for modern planning - data that the NSA has in hand.

Remember and Carry Away

For Americans, this should be a time when they should worry about their economic future and the short term and longer term future of the economy.

Worries should focus on the inability of saving the valuable economic institutions and the vitality that had been the cause of the dynamic growth that had characterized the economy prior to the year 2008.

The designed erosion and or systematic destruction of the economic processes which had made the US economic system the world's greatest - has reached a critical status for the launching of current Obama Administration to stop and/or slow down or reverse the degeneration of the competitive, capitalist system.

Without some rational interventional drive, it is certain to foster a demise of the economic role of government in its actions of error and failure to respond in a positive manner to lead to the viable future of the economy.

An immediate worry is how the Administration will act over the period until the election year of 2016.

If the previous eight years provide evidence or guidelines to predict the near term, a rational person would assume continued action to shift more and more economic control of the private sector to the central government. There is little evidence that since 2008 the economy has prospered.

Economic policies have not reversed the negative economic conditions. Not many positive situations have been a feature of the Administration's policies. Need to start for the period to 2016, including optimism or evidence under way to other policies that be used for economic problem solving.

Perhaps the legacy and means of control by Obama will be in the form of "central government planning" which would mean an extrapolation of the US transformation as a continuation of the failure of the Obama economic policies!

The advent of central planning as a logical and leftist mainstream administration is a plinth of the ideological basis of leftist economic policy and thought.

There is ample historical evidence that centralized government economic planning has been unsuccessful in many cases where it was tried and administered by an authoritarian one party or military regime.

Evidence of past failures is identified in this short book. Despite the absence of benefits from federalized economic decision making, modern leftists and a few communists continue to advocate such regimes and operations that we know about central government economic planning. You may feel a bit better informed about the pattern of errors and mistakes that characterize particular.

There was also an effort in coverage of information and materials to give and orientation or over view of the social and political attachments of planning systems.

The focus of many pages of this book has been on some of the social and political arrangements and institutions of planned economic systems.

As you end this particular encounter of exposition on planning, there are some other views that may help your understanding of the tribulations of establishing and indoctrinating such planning systems.

What follows is a short list of views as quotes from well informed bright people whose ideas about economics have persisted over the years.

The materialistic interpretation of history presupposes a dialectic process of development or progress---an unfolding process moving in terms of internal necessity toward a final goal.

Issues of economic policy are necessarily issues of politics. Even in theory it is difficult to distinguish between the economic and political aspects of a problem. Once the problem gets in the public arena, economics and politics are inextricably interwoven. Even if the economist tries to distinguish between the economic and political elements in his argument, the public is unlikely to recognize the distinction.

See T.W Hutchison, Positive Economics and Policy Objectives, Harvard University Press, 1964, page 197.

Interpretation of history

Also see Thorstein Veblen, A Critical Appraisal, edited by Douglas F. Dowd. Cornell University Press, 1958, page 138.

And more---

What appears to be a new development---arising out of situations in which the expertise pales when compared to the actualities and possibilities of unlighted individualism. of leading economists can be brushed aside as questionable or of dubious relevance—is the propensity of modern governments to invent their own bustard economics to justify their policies.

The State and the Economic System by Phyllis Deane Oxford University Press, 1988, page193.

And possibilities of enlightened individualism.

And----The dreams of socialists are but a bagatelle when compared to the actualities and possibilities of enlightened humans.

See Monopoly, by Vernon A. Mund. Princeton University Press, 1933, page 151.

the last---

…the basic problem of the twentieth century is the contradiction between an individual and collective interpretation of man….. The Western [non-communist world] world sees the individual human as part of the whole human being as the basic element of social and economic activity. In the Eastern [communist] world, man is seen as part of the whole. ...Here in the non-communist world it is expected that sensible action by the individual will lead to an optimum of communal well-being.

See Economic Philosophy of the Twentieth Century by Theo Surany-Unger. Northern Illinois University Press, 1968 Page 41.

As an ending thought in this reading, it can be assumed that the issues noted for the 20th Century continue to be politically debated in the 21st Century. The carry over as debates have been exacerbated by political dogma hog tied to an anachronistic philosophy linked to failed economic policies of years past as advocated by the leftist in a socialist regime and administration

Since 2008 the economy has not prospered. Economic policies have not reversed the negative economic conditions. Not many positive situations have been a feature of the Administration's polices. So at the start of has been used for economic problem solving. A few reticent cases where economic planning by the central government new year what economic conditions might be expected to get better of worse. Or in the bigger picture is it likely that the free enterprise, capitalistic system can be revitalized. Or is more likely that modifications to the market system will be eroded or replaced by alternatives such as central government economic planning? If you wish for change, that will come. But what changes. Some authorities predict a needed strengthening of the market system; other prognosticators assume that a larger more complete role of the federal government will be necessary.

What is included in the pages in this small book is a look at an upgrade on knowledge about the background and the effectiveness of policies based on the market as well as a review of the ineffective devices for economic management – identified as central government planning.

Appendix

The prior pages are a short rerun on planning from a book, "What's With the Economy" by VirtualBookWorm, Publishers, College Station, TX. Published in 2009. Author William L. Henderson. See particularly pages 308 - 314.

Some of the coverage could be considered repetitive--but approved by the author for inclusion in this attempt to have some understanding of the types of economic planning, The few pages of redundancy cover short takes on planning experience in China, Britain, France, and India with centralization overviews. FYI

Publisher:

ICOM Multimedia
ISBN:
978-0-9851022-3-4